FACT FRENZY
SPACE

ASTRONAUT LIFE

Lisa Regan

PowerKiDS press

Published in 2021 by
The Rosen Publishing Group, Inc.
29 East 21st Street, New York, NY 10010

Cataloging-in-Publication Data

Names: Regan, Lisa.
Title: Astronaut life / Lisa Regan.
Description: New York : PowerKids Press, 2021. | Series:
Fact frenzy: space | Includes glossary and index.
Identifiers: ISBN 9781725320123 (pbk.) | ISBN
9781725320147 (library bound) | ISBN 9781725320130
(6 pack)
Subjects: LCSH: Astronauts--Juvenile literature. | Manned
space flight--Juvenile literature. | Space sciences--Juvenile
literature. | Outer space--Exploration--Juvenile literature.
Classification: LCC TL793.R465 2021 | DDC 629.45--dc23

Manufactured in the United States of America

CPSIA Compliance Information: Batch CSPK20: For Further Information contact
Rosen Publishing, New York, New York at 1-800-237-9932.

Find us on

Contents

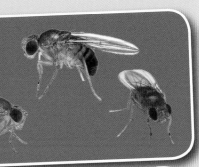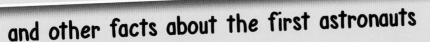

THE FIRST ANIMALS IN SPACE WERE FRUIT FLIES

Two fruit flies were launched into space in a rocket in 1947. The rocket just passed over the Kármán Line, 60 miles (100 km) above Earth's surface, which is considered the start of space.

This is one small flight for flies, one giant leap for flykind!

There's no fruit in space, so what are we going to eat?!

Flying high

As humans, we think pretty highly of ourselves compared with other animals. But despite all our cleverness, the humble fruit fly beat us into space! Scientists wanted to check how safe space travel was for humans, so they sent up two fruit flies in a rocket to see what happened to them. Luckily for the flies, they came safely back down to Earth and survived to fly another day!

FACT **2**

A number of animals have been bred in space, including jellyfish, frogs, and sea urchins.

Why fruit flies?

You wouldn't think that humans and fruit flies have a lot in common, but actually we're more similar than we look! Our genes contain information about our bodies and what they do, and over 60% of disease-causing genes in humans have recognizable matches in fruit flies. This means that looking at how fruit flies are affected by space travel can tell us quite a lot about what might happen to humans.

Weightless apes

Before humans went up into space, scientists were very concerned that we may not survive long periods of weightlessness. We share about 99% of our genetic code—our DNA—with chimpanzees, so in 1961, U.S. scientists launched a chimpanzee named Ham into space to see how it would affect him. He returned safe and well, just a little tired and thirsty. This mission paved the way for the first successful human astronaut launch later that year.

IN 1973, A SPIDER SPUN THE FIRST EVER WEB IN SPACE.

Animal heroes

Many other animals have been launched into space, including dogs, mice, rats, rabbits, insects, tortoises, fish, frogs, jellyfish, snails, and spiders. Sadly, some of these animals did not survive, and we owe them a huge amount in helping us understand how to make space travel safe for humans. Scientists have continued to test how space affects animals in different ways, and what long-term effects space travel might have on humans.

Ham, the chimpanzee astronaut.

A Russian stamp dedicated to Laika, the first dog in space.

PEOPLE THOUGHT ASTRONAUTS MIGHT GET SPACE DISEASES

When astronauts first went into space in the 1960s, scientists were worried that they might bring back deadly new diseases and tiny alien creatures.

I'm fine, honest!

The *Apollo 11* astronauts, meeting President Nixon while still being kept in isolation.

Moon sickness

When the crew of *Apollo 11* returned to Earth after landing on the moon for the first time, they were not allowed back out into the world for 21 days. They stayed in a secure area undergoing a range of different tests. Scientists had no idea what diseases or alien life-forms they might have accidentally brought back with them, and didn't want to risk exposing Earth to new and mysterious dangers from space.

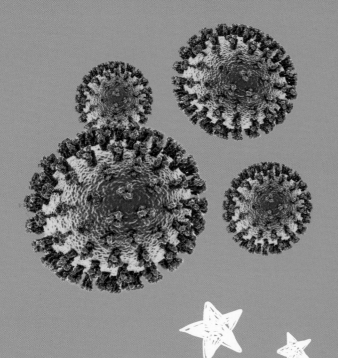

Sharing space

NASA's worries make sense—even between different countries on Earth, introducing new life-forms can cause huge problems. Imagine what could happen with life from beyond Earth! When Europeans first came to the Americas, they brought diseases—such as smallpox and influenza—that killed many local people whose bodies had no resistance to them. Australia's plants and animals have also been badly affected by people bringing in species that do not naturally exist in the country.

Moon rocks

The Apollo crews also brought back quite a large amount of material from the moon, and this could also have carried dangerous or deadly life-forms. NASA scientists kept the moon rocks in a secure space with different species of animals to make sure that they weren't poisonous or harmful in any way. They fed cockroaches moon rock and also used shrimp, oysters, and houseflies to test their safety.

A piece of rock from the moon.

Safety first

The *Apollo 12* and *Apollo 14* crews (*Apollo 13* wasn't able to land on the moon) were also kept apart from others and tested in the same way when they returned to Earth. After this, scientists were convinced that there was no life on the moon to attach itself to astronauts and pose a risk to life on Earth. People returning from space are now allowed to return home right away, after some health checks.

ASTRONAUTS CAN'T BURP IN SPACE

When people are in space, gas and liquids don't separate in their stomachs as they do on Earth. You can't burp without being sick!

No upside-down burping!

When you burp, you send gas from your stomach out of your mouth. You can do this without vomiting because gases are lighter than liquids and solids, so the gas sits at the top of your stomach. If you turned upside down and tried to burp, the gas would have risen upward toward your feet, so it would be in the wrong place. You would vomit instead of burping!

Uh-oh, guess I better hold it in until we're back home!

Soda bubbles

In space, though, astronauts experience what we call microgravity because they are in constant free fall toward Earth. Nothing is heavier than anything else in free fall, so gases don't rise above liquids or solids. Imagine a glass of soda. The bubbles within the liquid rush toward the top of the glass and escape, right? But in microgravity, the bubbles stay inside the liquid and don't move upward. The same thing happens with gas in your stomach in space.

In space, these bubbles would never reach the top!

FACT 5

Astronauts' feet get baby soft in space because they don't walk on the ground and the rough skin falls off.

Astronaut Sunita Williams exercising aboard the International Space Station.

Floating liquids

Liquids are always moving through our bodies. When we are on Earth, gravity helps to move these liquids downward. In microgravity this doesn't happen, so the liquids rise toward the head. NASA found that over the year that astronaut Scott Kelly spent in space, around 3.5 pints (2,000 ml) of fluid shifted into his head.

Space workouts

Space travel isn't great for your health. Your body has to work quite hard against gravity when you're on Earth just to stay upright and move around, and in microgravity astronauts' muscles quickly waste away from not being used enough as they float around. To avoid this, astronauts have to exercise for around two hours a day.

CRYING IN SPACE COULD KILL YOU

Your eyes can form tears in space, but because there is no gravity the tears won't fall. They just make a big liquid bubble on your face. This can be very bad news ...

Dangerous tears

Andrew Feustel found out the hard way how risky crying in space can be. While he was on a spacewalk outside the International Space Station, a flake of the solution used to defog the inside of his spacesuit helmet got in his eye. It stung, so his eye reacted naturally and started watering to try to flush out the irritation. But crying doesn't work like that in space.

Nooo, I can't see!

Blinded in space

As Andrew's eye pushed out tears, a liquid bubble formed and spread across his face and into his other eye. The tears stung painfully and meant he couldn't see anything at all, but there was very little anyone could do. Which is not what you want to hear when, as Andrew was, you are floating in space holding a power drill!

Happy ending

Luckily, after some time, Andrew eventually managed to move inside his spacesuit to rub his eye on a sticking-out piece of foam. He finished his spacewalk and returned safely to the International Space Station (ISS). Inside the ISS, astronauts don't have to wear spacesuits with helmets, so although tears bubble on your face in the same way, it's less of an issue as you can use your hands to brush them away. You can even watch them float in front of you!

WE HAVE TEARS IN OUR EYES ALL THE TIME TO KEEP THEM MOIST—THEY ARE CALLED BASAL TEARS.

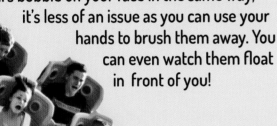

Microgravity

The reason that tears do not fall inside or outside the ISS is not because there is no gravity. In fact, the ISS is so close to Earth that it still has 90% gravity. The reason is microgravity—the same reason you feel like you're flying just as a rollercoaster drops downward. As gravity pulls the ISS toward Earth, other forces pull it sideways, so rather than crashing down to Earth it free falls around our planet in a constant circle.

SPACE SMELLS LIKE STEAK AND BURNING METAL

Astronauts agree that space smells ... funny. People describe it differently, but most agree that it is at once sweet, sharp, and metallic.

Bringing in a smell

Have you ever brought anything smelly into the house on your shoes? Don't worry, so have astronauts! Astronaut Don Pettit has said that his fellow astronauts carried in a "space smell" with them when they returned from spacewalks. Whenever he opened the hatch on the spacecraft to bring the astronauts back in, he noticed their spacesuits, gloves, helmets, and even their tools smelled odd—but it took him a while to figure out why!

SCIENTISTS BELIEVE HUMANS CAN RECOGNIZE 1 TRILLION DIFFERENT SMELLS.

Sugar and rotten eggs

Our solar system may be especially smelly. We have lots of carbon in our solar system and not much oxygen, giving it a strong and sooty smell. Think of an old car that gives off lots of nasty smoke from its exhaust—nice! We could have it worse—solar systems with lots of sulfur may smell like rotten eggs. On the other hand, it could be better, as scientists think some solar systems smell sugary sweet!

Ew, who would have thought our solar system stunk like an old car?!

Astronaut smells

With up to six living, breathing human beings living aboard the International Space Station at any one time, things could get a bit smelly, especially as no one can have a shower or do laundry properly in space. There is a built-in system for clearing smells, but astronauts have said they sometimes got annoyed with each other for leaving sweaty workout clothes around and cooking smelly food!

Smell science

NASA has thought about trying to recreate the smell of space on Earth, talking to scientists about how they might be able to do this. The reason isn't just their curiosity—going into space is an exciting but often overwhelming experience, so in NASA's training program they try to prepare people as fully as they can for their trip. This includes recreating sights, sounds, and maybe even smells.

FACT 9

You can't do laundry in space, so dirty clothes are destroyed. They are sent down to Earth in a disposable spacecraft that burns up in the atmosphere, over the ocean.

SPACE TRAVEL CAN CHANGE YOUR BODY FOREVER

Astronaut Scott Kelly spent a year in the International Space Station. When he came back, scientists found that some interesting changes had taken place inside his body.

Scott and Mark Kelly

Twin astronauts

Scott Kelly has an identical twin brother, Mark, who is also an astronaut. As their DNA is almost identical, scientists can run some very interesting experiments looking at how each brother's DNA is affected by experiences in space. After Scott spent a year in space, many newspaper reports said his DNA had changed so much that he and Mark—who had remained on Earth—were no longer identical. It's a great headline, but it's not quite right ...

FACT 11

Space can cause astronauts' eyes to change in ways that can cause vision problems and possibly even blindness.

Do I look different?

16

Switching genes

Genes are segments of our DNA, the code written into our body's cells that describe how we look and many other things about us. We inherit our genes from our parents, but different conditions or events in our lives can cause them to "switch" on and off and affect our body in different ways. What you eat, where you live, when you sleep, and all sorts of other things can trigger these on/off changes.

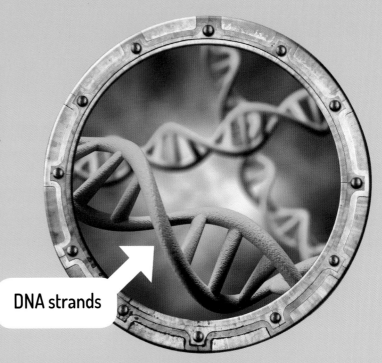

DNA strands

Permanent change

As you might imagine, going into space is quite an unusual thing for a person to do. However exciting it may be, it also puts a lot of physical stress on the body. It can cause genes to switch on and off, sometimes permanently so. While Scott was in space and Mark remained on Earth, Scott's genes switched on and off in different ways and it looks like around 7% of these changes are irreversible.

Bodies in space

Other changes are temporary—for instance, scientists found that Scott was taller than when he'd left, because the lower gravity in space meant his spine wasn't pulled down toward Earth as much. This happens to everyone in space, and they usually return to their pre-space height within ten days.

17

YOUR PHONE COULD POWER THE MOON LANDING

Smartphones today are far more powerful than the supercomputers of the past, which launched rockets into space in the 1960s and put men on the moon.

Genius phones

A smartphone is an incredible piece of technology. It does the job of an address book, a calculator, an alarm clock, a map, a music player, a payment card, a bus ticket, and so many more things. It's not just a phone, it's a brilliantly fast and versatile computer that we carry around in our pocket—and it performs instructions hundreds of million times faster than the best computers used in the Apollo moon missions.

Texting? Don't you know I could send you to space?!

Back in time

It's easy to forget that when we first landed on the moon in 1969, the very first general-purpose, programmable electronic computer had only been completed 23 years earlier. It was called ENIAC, and the U.S. began building it during World War II. It eventually took up around 1,800 square feet (167 sq m) of space—about the size of seven buses! It weighed around 30 tons, as much as five elephants.

Faster, stronger, smarter

By the time of the first Apollo space missions in the 1960s, computers were more advanced, and they kept evolving over the following decades. As we moved into the new millennium, though, this rate of development kicked up to turbo speed. Technology has developed so quickly that even "smart" refrigerators and microwaves have more computing power than any of the computers NASA used to help put people on the moon!

Super programmers

The usefulness of a computer isn't just about its raw power, though—it depends on programmers working out how to give the computer its instructions. Margaret Hamilton, a NASA programmer on the Apollo missions, has said that it was like working in the "Wild West"—there weren't really many rules yet, they just had to make it up and try it! These programmers' genius and creativity helped harness the computers' limited power to do incredible things.

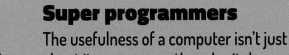

Margaret Hamilton and the software that powered the Apollo project.

FOOTPRINTS ON THE MOON STAY THERE FOREVER

There is no water or wind on the moon to sweep away footprints on its surface. This means that astronauts' footprints may last as long as the moon itself.

FACT 14

The word astronaut comes from the Greek words "astron" (star) and "nautes" (sailor).

Walking on the moon

Twenty-four people have flown to the moon and twelve people have actually walked on its surface. The most famous are the first two to walk on the moon's surface: Neil Armstrong and Buzz Aldrin. They flew there on the *Apollo 11* mission, first stepping out onto the moon on July 20, 1969. They spent over 21 hours on its surface, but less than three hours outside of the landing spacecraft.

Just look at all these footprints!

Moon littering

It isn't just footprints that humans have left on the moon. For a start, there are hundreds of pieces of spacecraft wreckage. Visiting astronauts have also left things behind, including two golf balls, 12 pairs of boots; empty food packets, 12 cameras (the film was brought back to Earth), and a single falcon feather dropped alongside a hammer to prove they would hit the ground at the same time.

Moon memorials

Other objects left on the moon are meant to remain on its surface as symbolic reminders for all time. Some have to do with peace, such as a golden olive branch and a disk with messages of goodwill from leaders of 73 countries. Others are about space travel itself, including a 3-inch (8.5 cm) "fallen astronaut" sculpture that remembers those who have died for the cause of space exploration.

NO ONE HAS EVER WALKED ON THE MOON MORE THAN ONCE.

Surviving the sun?

Although footprints and objects are not swept away by water or wind, they are also not protected from the sun by Earth's atmosphere. The U.S. flags left behind are bleached white from the sun now, as is the family photo left on the moon's surface by astronaut Charles Duke.

The Fallen Astronaut sculpture in front of a memorial plaque.

Charles Duke in front of a picture of himself walking on the moon.

Time moves faster in space than on Earth because the Earth's orbit gives us an extra second per week. This means astronauts time travel as they move between space and Earth.

Space clocks

The existence of this extra time on Earth is called "time dilation" and it has been proven over and over again by taking very accurate clocks on trips into space. We can compare the time on two clocks—one in space and one on Earth—and see the difference between them. Scientists have also recorded the time difference between a pair of clocks after one of them had been in space.

> I want my 100 millionths of a second back!

Einstein time

Famous scientist Albert Einstein "realized" that time isn't always the same—it depends on where you are. This isn't just true for space, though. Being higher up on Earth also means that you experience time as faster. If you spent your whole life at the top of a 100-floor skyscraper, you would lose around 100 millionths of a second of your life. Scientists have used clocks that are accurate to within one second over 3.7 billion years to show this on Earth.

Travel to the future

Russian cosmonaut Sergei Krikalev has spent more time orbiting around the Earth than anyone else—a total of 803 days, 9 hours, and 39 minutes. This means he's completed more time travel than anyone else on Earth. As he still lives in the same time frame as everyone else on Earth, it is as if he has gone 0.02 seconds into his own future.

Science fiction

Along with invisibility and being able to fly, time travel is something that many people would love to do. But is it possible on a larger scale—days, months, years? Many scientists think so, although it's much more complicated to think about how to travel into the past than into the future. We are still only beginning to understand how things work differently elsewhere in space compared to on Earth, and what incredible things that might make possible.

A trip to the past? Maybe someday ...

A MAN'S ASHES ARE BURIED ON THE MOON

Dr. Eugene Shoemaker was a brilliant scientist who helped to train astronauts going to the moon. After his death, some of his ashes were carried to the moon in 1999 and remain there to this day.

Eugene Shoemaker and his wife, Carolyn, spotted comets that had never been recorded before.

Groundbreaking scientist

Shoemaker was a geologist, a scientist who studies rocks. He devoted his life to space, looking at the different objects—such as moons, comets, and planets—in our solar system and how they were formed. He was a world-renowned expert in craters on Earth, other planets, and the moon, and he trained astronauts to explore the moon's rocks and craters in a scientific way. He also discovered several comets, which are named after him.

Shoemaker could never join astronauts on the moon—not during his lifetime, anyway.

Astronaut dreams

Shoemaker had a lifelong dream to travel into space—and, above all, to go to the moon. He was all set to be the first geologist to ever walk on the moon, but tests at NASA found that he had a health condition which meant it wasn't considered safe for him to go. Although he had an incredible scientific career filled with important achievements and awards, he was always haunted by his now-impossible dream.

Craters and comets

Shoemaker had a rich life exploring craters all over the world, often with his wife and fellow scientist Carolyn Shoemaker. It was on such a trip to Australia that he sadly died in a car accident while driving to a remote crater. Shortly before Shoemaker died, he said, "Not going to the moon ... has been the biggest disappointment in life." But, as we know, his friends and family would put that right in his death.

Finally at peace

Shoemaker's ashes were carried to their final resting place on the moon in a capsule etched with pictures of Comet Hale-Bopp, the last comet that he ever saw with his wife, and a quotation from Shakespeare's play Romeo and Juliet. Although some people have paid to launch their remains into space, Shoemaker is the only person buried anywhere else beyond Earth. His wife said, "We will always know when we look at the moon, that he is there."

The quote on Shoemaker's ashes capsule reads:

And, when he shall die
Take him and cut him out in little stars
And he will make the face of heaven so fine
That all the world will be in love with night
And pay no worship to the garish sun.

EVEN MORE FACTS!

You've found out lots about exploring space, but there's always more to discover! Boost your knowledge here with even more facts.

On August 15, 1950, a mouse was launched into space inside a rocket and reached an altitude of 85 miles (137 km). Unfortunately, the mouse died on its way down when the rocket's parachute failed.

"Astronaut" comes from the Greek words "astron nautes," which means "star sailor." In Russia and the former Soviet Union, astronauts are called "cosmonauts," from the Greek words "kosmos nautes," meaning "universe sailor."

The first human to travel into outer space was Yuri Gagarin (1934–1968), a Russian cosmonaut who successfully orbited Earth over the course of 108 minutes in the *Vostok 1* spacecraft, on April 12, 1961.

The first American in space was Alan Shepherd (1923–1998), who entered space on the *Freedom 7* spacecraft, three weeks after Yuri Gagarin. On February 20, 1962, John Glenn (1921–2016) became the first American to orbit Earth on the *Friendship 7* spacecraft.

The first woman in space was Russian cosmonaut Valentina Tereshkova, who left Earth on June 16, 1963, at the age of 26. Tereshkova's radio call sign was Chaika, meaning "Seagull." Once in space, she radioed to Earth, "It is I, Seagull! I see the horizon; it's a sky blue with a dark strip. How beautiful the Earth is."

When astronaut Neil Armstrong (1930–2012) first stepped onto the Moon on July 20, 1969, he made the famous statement, "That's one small step for a man, one giant leap for mankind."

Buzz Aldrin (b.1930) was the second person to walk on the moon. Aldrin was the pilot of the lunar module called *Eagle*, which landed on the moon on July 20, 1969. He stepped onto the moon 19 minutes after Neil Armstrong.

In 1983, Sally Ride (1951–2012) became the first American woman in space as a crew member of the *Challenger*. She was one of only 35 people out of 8,000 applicants that NASA selected to join a new class of astronauts.

Between 1955 and 1975, the U.S. and Russia raced to explore space in a period called the Space Race. Russia got the first person in space, and the U.S. the first person on the moon. The Space Race ended when both countries worked together on the Apollo–Soyuz project.

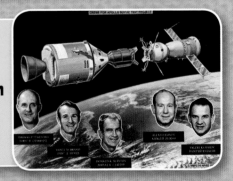

There are six American flags on the moon, but this doesn't mean it belongs to the U.S. An international law written in 1967, two years before Armstrong set foot on the moon, prevents any single country from owning planets, moons, or stars in space.

ASTRONAUT LIFE GLOSSARY

Apollo A space program consisting of manned U.S. spacecraft designed to explore the moon and surrounding space.

astronaut A person trained for traveling in a spacecraft.

atmosphere A shell of gases kept around a planet, star, or other object by its gravity.

call sign The letters or numbers that identify someone using a radio for communication.

carbon A chemical element that occurs in carbon dioxide, coal, and oil.

comet A chunk of rock and ice from the edge of the solar system.

cosmonaut An astronaut from the former Soviet Union.

crater A very large hole in the ground, created by something hitting it or by an explosion.

DNA An acid in the center of the cells of living things that is responsible for characteristics being passed on from parents to their children.

free fall The descent of a body in which gravity is the only force acting on it.

genes The part of the cell in a living thing that controls its physical characteristics, growth, and development.

genetic code The order in which the bases of DNA are arranged in a molecule.

gravity A natural force created around objects with mass, which draws other objects toward them.

International Space Station (ISS) A space station launched in 1998 with the cooperation of 16 nations. The ISS orbits Earth for scientific and space research.

Kármán Line An imaginary boundary where space begins, or the border between Earth's atmosphere and outer space. It is 60 miles (100 km) above sea level.

lunar module A vehicle for traveling from a spacecraft to the surface of the moon and back to the spacecraft.

microgravity Very weak gravity, as you would find inside a spacecraft circling around Earth.

millenium A period of 1,000 years.

moon Earth's closest companion in space, a ball of rock that orbits Earth every 27.3 days. Most other planets in the solar system have moons of their own.

NASA An abbreviation for "National Aeronautics and Space Administration," the American government organization concerned with spacecraft and space travel.

orbit A fixed path taken by one object in space around another because of the effect of gravity.

oxygen A colorless gas that exists in large quantities in the air, and which is needed by all plants and animals to survive.

planet A world, orbiting a star, which has enough mass and gravity to pull itself into a ball-like shape, and clear space around it of other large objects.

solar system The eight planets (including Earth) and their moons, and other objects such as asteroids, that orbit around the sun.

Soviet Union A former republic in Eastern Europe and Northern Asia, under Communist rule, that broke up in 1991.

spacecraft A vehicle that travels into space.

spacesuit A sealed and pressurized suit worn by astronauts that provides the correct temperature, radio communication, and protection from radiation for work outside a spacecraft.

spacewalk When an astronaut leaves the spacecraft and works outside it while floating in space.

species A group of plants or animals that have the same main characteristics and are able to breed with each other.

sulfur A yellow chemical that has a strong smell.

supercomputers Powerful computers that can process large quantities of data very quickly.

FURTHER INFORMATION

BOOKS

Aguilar, David. *Space Encyclopedia.* London, UK: National Geographic Kids, 2013.

Becklade, Sue. *Wild About Space.* Thaxted, UK: Miles Kelly, 2020.

Betts, Bruce. *Astronomy for Kids: How to Explore Outer Space with Binoculars, a Telescope, or Just Your Eyes!* Emeryville, CA: Rockridge Press, 2018.

DK. *The Astronomy Book: Big Ideas Simply Explained.* London, UK: DK, 2017.

DK. *Knowledge Encyclopedia Space!: The Universe as You've Never Seen It Before.* London, UK: DK, 2015.

Frith, Alex, Jerome Martin, and Alice James. *100 Things to Know About Space.* London, UK: Usborne Publishing, 2016.

National Geographic Kids. *Everything: Space.* London, UK: Collins, 2018.

WEBSITES

Ducksters Astronomy for Kids
http://www.ducksters.com/science/astronomy.php
Head to this website to find out all there is to know about astronomy; you can also try an astronomy crossword puzzle and word search!

NASA Science: Space Place
https://spaceplace.nasa.gov
Discover all sorts of facts about space, other planets, and the moon. You can even play the Mars Rover Game, sending commands to the Mars rover and collecting as much data as possible in eight expeditions!

Science Kids: Space for Kids
http://www.sciencekids.co.nz/space.html
Go beyond our planet and explore space through fun facts, games, videos, quizzes, and projects.

Publisher's note to educators and parents: Our editors have carefully reviewed these websites to ensure that they are suitable for students. Many websites change frequently, however, and we cannot guarantee that a site's future contents will continue to meet our high standards of quality and educational value. Be advised that students should be closely supervised whenever they access the Internet.

INDEX